Lessons from the Universe

Poems of Enlightenment

Lessons from the Universe

Poems of Enlightenment

Stevie Ray Robison

Living the Poem Publishing
110 South Bedford Street
Suite B
Georgetown, Delaware, US 19947
www.livingthepoem.com

Copyright © 2010 Steve Robison

All Rights Reserved. No part of this book may be reproduced or used in any manner without the written (inclusive of email) permission of the publisher, except for short excerpts used for the purpose of marketing or review of this book.

Cover photo by Steve Robison

ISBN: 1453815740
EAN-13: 978-1453815748

Dedicated to Elizma. Your words of inspired encouragement came at just the right moment. I am deeply appreciative.

My hands rest on the canvas of my dreams. I am the composer and the artist and the symphony and the painting. Moving deftly, slowly, clumsily, recklessly, thoughtfully – moving, moving, moving. My hands were made to write the songs of my heart, my heart was made to sing the songs of the universe. The universe was made to dance the dance of life with me.

My hands rest on the crux of realization, connecting heart, soul, mind, atom, galaxy, thought, and word. Let the dreams forever flow, freely and powerfully; let the majesty of life move my hands to write.

Table of Contents

Introduction – What is Enlightenment?....1

Chapter 1 – Glimpses..........................5

    Come, Dear Children............................6

    Out of the Mire...................................8

    Blank..9

    Dreamer..10

    The Grander Image...........................11

    The Way..12

    Foundation..13

    Clothed in Divine...............................14

    Return to Innocence.........................15

    This Morning....................................16

    Three Signs......................................18

Chapter 2 – The Walk........................19

    Mountains of Destiny........................20

A Short Walk 21

Searching..27

Seeking..28

An Act of Kindness................................29

Walking Today.......................................30

Through the Wrath................................31

Reflections...32

Thankfulness...33

The Softer Way......................................34

Circuitous Meanderings........................35

This Moment...36

Final Song's Hopeful Dawn..................37

Manners...38

Washed Away..39

Universal Truths....................................40

Moved..42

Quiet Suddenness, Return to Grace...........45

Choices on the Path..............................46

Wonders...47

Chapter 3 – Heaven..................................49

    Together..................................50

    Instant of Perfection..................................51

    Flowing Divine..................................52

    Just Beneath..................................54

    Angel's Song..................................55

    Pleased..................................56

    Empty Vessel..................................57

    Deeper..................................58

    Brightened Skies..................................60

    Resting..................................61

Chapter 4 – Love..................................63

    Grace's Invitation..................................64

    Love's Message..................................65

    Earthen Beginnings..................................66

    Humble Me..................................67

    Transformed..................................69

    Newfound Joy..................................70

    Inside..................................71

    To Lead...72

    A Hint of New Beginnings.........................73

    Living in the Midst..................................74

    Emigrant...75

    Glorious Love..77

    Pursuit..78

Chapter 5 – One.....................................79

    Charisma..80

    Peaceful Moment's Knowing......................81

    One Heart...82

    They Smiled..83

    As One..85

    Sacred Connected Whole........................86

    Holy Unity..87

    Return Again..88

    Here and Now...89

    Seven Rungs on the Ladder of Love.............91

Chapter 6 - Leap....................................93

    All..94

Glory, Divine..96

Emerge..97

Quiet Walk..98

A Single Tear...100

Genuine Perfection..102

Dark Corners...103

Alloy..104

Reawakened..106

Ancient Surrender...107

Chapter 7 – Revelation..................................109

Mystic Truths..110

Useful Quest..111

New Century...112

The Three Voices..113

He Knew..114

Quest for Peace...115

Birthing Creation's Power.............................116

Grief's Abandonment....................................117

Manifest Gratitude..119

Replace...120

Life Flows..121

The Cluttered Closet..........................122

Perfect Mindfulness...........................124

Return..125

Fruit and Seed....................................126

Chapter 8 – Into the Light...................127

Gloriously Reawakened.....................128

New Arrivals.......................................129

Thy Kingdom Come............................130

Red, Violet, Indigo.............................131

Life Moves On....................................132

Unbending the Light..........................133

Angel...134

Beneath the Surface..........................135

The Lost Secrets................................137

Child of Perfection.............................140

Synergistic..141

Sharing the Dream............................142

Creation's Frantic Dance............................143

Chapter 9 – Beyond............................145

Unforetold..146

Peace, Love, Nirvana............................147

Essence of Grief......................................148

Parallels..149

Sacred Meditation of Ecstasy...................151

Falling...154

Time's Creative Moment..........................156

Beyond a Moment...................................157

Intersecting..158

Dark Skies..159

Retreating...160

Dark Silence...162

Introduction – What is Enlightenment?

The word enlightenment has many meanings and interpretations. Its use has become widespread with the increase in the accessibility of knowledge, information, and communication media.

To some, it is the highest level of spiritual development and understanding. The enlightened beings, it is believed, have no limits whatever, and freely move from this realm to others and back, or exist in all realms simultaneously. With access to the fullness of wisdom and knowledge of the Universe, which they are mindfully and completely aware of, nothing is beyond the thought or reach of these enlightened ones.

To others, there are various levels of enlightenment, rungs on a ladder of personal and universal evolution. These seek to grow through study, practice, and living, increasing their level of enlightenment with their higher levels of thought and action.

And to still others, being enlightened is simply being aware of the "Light", the Universal Everpresent It that encompasses all.

Your definition and interpretation matters little for the purpose of this collection of enlightened writings. Its aim is simple, to guide you, the reader, to, in, or toward states of higher awareness.

Enjoy!

Chapter 1 – Glimpses

Come, Dear Children

Standing by the still and quiet waters
Calling to mind the greatness of your gifts
Choosing to surrender more deeply
We draw in a breath and dive in

As ripples lap at the shore of truth
Gently, we swim toward the unknown depths
Dark and unfamiliar is the way of faith
Warm and familiar, your encouraging voice

> *Come, dear children*
> *My Way is clear*
> *In peace forever*
> *Unstrap your fear*
>
> *Bound no more*
> *Live in The Way*
> *In peace forever*
> *Starting this day*
>
> *My love is here*
> *Present and real*
> *To open eyes*
> *I shall reveal*
>
> *Come, dear children*

Stevie Ray Robison

These words, sincere
Let me guide you
My Way is clear

As we wake in peace from the dream
Perfect Light feeds each glorious soul
Alive and clear, in oneness now
You and I and God are whole

Out of the Mire

Out of the mire
Lotus rises true
From yesterday's sorrows
Hope springs forth anew

Out of the east
Colors call your name
Echoes of tomorrow
Today ringing the same

Fearful frustration
Ego's lonely call
Trudging the miles
Walking ever tall

Healing and sickness
Sorrow and great glee
Walk the path of clarity
Open eyes still see

Out of the mire
Lotus rises true
From yesterday's sorrows
Hope springs forth anew

Stevie Ray Robison

Blank

A blank sheet of music
The song at your command
Lyrics, notes, and chords
Chosen by your hand

Write your heart's own song
Stand and dance your dance
Discover your inheritance
Choose to take the chance

Flowing from within
River of endless time
Taste the joyful waters
And rhyme another rhyme

Song of your creation
Choose to make it great
Write it from your heart
And live your glorious fate

Dreamer

Moss grows on the tree
Stealing its best life force
End of time is nearing
Moment of rest at hand

Eyes refuse to open
Dreaming of the coming dream
Deafening silent refrains
Echoes from a waiting mind

Stage is all set, players arrive
Be the dreamer's dream
Alive in the bliss of fantasy
Nothing is quite as it seems

Desperately, succinctly, longingly
Moving toward the truth
Living in the dream
Walking to the edge

The Grander Image

In the grander image
Perspective changes
And all time and space
Collapse into the void

In the higher realities
Absolute truths come into focus
Time does not exist
All events occur in nowness

From Divinity's eyes
All spirits are One
Love is God
And God is Love

The Way

Tempered by the lessons
Strengthened by the storm
In the power and the refuge
Let the God of all transform

Touched by holy fire
Living in this dark place
Peace and joy result
When mind is one with grace

If love is all there is
Then live in love today
Enduring love's new trials
Each moment in the Way

Stevie Ray Robison

Foundation

Strengthen this foundation
Further and deeper indeed
Dig within these hearts
Plant your holy seeds

Help us to stand tall
In you, all blessings live
Teacher, guide our hearts
Grant us the power to give

The deeper, God, you dig
Deeper the foundation is poured
In time, we'll raise the building
With love and trust restored

Clothed in Divine

Remove from me this feeling
That seeps into my mind
Fill me in your presence
Clothe me in divine

Human frailty blooms
Touched by judgment's rain
Unaccepted child
Filled in old disdain

Burn away the suffering
Wash away the pain
Flood me in your healing love
Let not peace now wane

Take me to the altar
Sacrifice my life
End the rising tide
Burn away the strife

Remove from me this feeling
That seeps into my mind
Fill me in your presence
Clothe me in divine

Return to Innocence

Confusion is seeded
In thoughts that impede
The flowing of knowledge
A tall growing weed

Confused and alone
Illusions of loss
Forgetting the reason
Forgetting the cost

A child is born
In perfection, indeed
Wanting for nothing
Having no need

So, return to the innocence
Of a wondering child
Wander no more
Be today, reconciled

This Morning

I woke this morning
And felt a gentle breeze
I woke this morning
And heard a bird's song

You woke this morning
I breathed you a breeze
You woke this morning
I sang a gentle song

I woke this morning
Heard your unspeakable name
I woke this morning
And would never be the same

You woke this morning
I smiled as I called your name
You woke this morning
We will never be the same

I woke this morning
And felt a gentle breeze
I woke this morning
And felt the Spirit's pull

You woke this morning, child

Stevie Ray Robison

And caused me to smile in delight
You woke this new morning
What a glorious and wondrous sight

Three Signs

Three hawks soar above
Into the bright setting sun
A sign of the most holy moment
Knowing the perfection of one

Three souls look from below
Admire the majesty of flight
A sign of the most holy moment
Knowing the presence of light

Three leaves fall from the tree
Gently on gentle moving winds
A sign of the most holy moment
Knowing where new life begins

Three signs of the dawning of truth
Seen by a seeker of more
Learning the lessons presented
There's no need to seek anymore

Chapter 2 – The Walk

Mountains of Destiny

Every dawning moment
Is a gateway to choice
Future moments riding
On a journey of actions

Starting with a thought
Affected by intent
Each step is taken
In a walk of this life

Find your highest thought
Take your highest action
Lean on a trusted God
Climb the mountains of destiny

Stevie Ray Robison

A Short Walk

I am love
As you are love
It is all we know

These words
Simple, yet profound
Have become
And are becoming
Our truth
Our reality
Our existence

There was a time
Not so many years ago
When we walked
Through the valley
Of twisted souls
Of lost dreams
Of bitter tastes
Of loveless light

Rising high above
This valley below
The peaks
Rose in majestic beauty
Hinted at a new path

A path of peace
A path of love
Beckoned us

The path was steep
Rocky
Perilous
Treacherous

We could not carry
All of the burdens
We once carried
As we climbed
The ever-steepening path
Toward a peak
We desired to reach
We needed to reach

So, as we walked
Hiked
Climbed
Toward our destiny
Toward the truths of the heights
Toward the blinding lights
As we walked
We left behind
Everything

We left everything on the path

Stevie Ray Robison

As we walked on
As we trekked on
As we journeyed on

Each step
Was one step closer
Each step
Led us toward the peak
The pinnacle
The prize
Wisdom
Love
Understanding
Enlightenment

Many, many times
We stumbled
Occasionally losing ground
But we walked on
We walked on

Many, many times
We questioned
Occasionally losing faith
But we walked on
We walked on

Every day we walked
And every day we paused

Reflecting
Recalling
The quest
The need
The purpose

Love was at the peak
Peace was at the peak
Light was at the peak
Home was at the peak
The peak was where we needed to be

We walked on
Through the trials
Through the tears
Through the doubts
We walked on

Dropping our burdens
Confronting our fears
And dropping them, too
One at a time
One step at a time
We walked on

The journey
Was sometimes solitary
But other times
We were joined

Stevie Ray Robison

For a word
For a lesson
For a time
For a moment
We walked on

We chose to walk this path
We choose to walk this path
We choose it again and again
Because we must

When others hurt us
We walk on
When others leave
We walk on
When others misunderstand us
We attempt to help them to see
And then
We walk on

On the path of awareness
On this path that is our destiny
There are obstacles
There are perils
There is pain
There is sorrow
There is loss
There are tears
But also

Lessons from the Universe – Poems of Enlightenment

There is love

I am love
As you are love
It is all we know

And so
We walk on
We walk on

Searching

Searching for love
Grasping for peace
Clinging to fear
Needing release

Gratitude lost
Suffering found
Heaven's gate left
Hell's furnace bound

Holding on tight
To misery and loss
Path of the ego
Whatever the cost

Surrender once more
Accept holy grace
Call out His name
Seek now His face

Seeking

Seeking bliss
Bliss, we find
Seek light
Receive divine

Seeking sorrow
Sorrow found
Misery travels
Pain abounds

Sowing hope
Truth and peace
Reap the harvest
Loving feast

Stevie Ray Robison

An Act of Kindness

An act of gentle kindness
Touches a warrior's core
Soothing spring rains
Covering, drenching, pure

Melting the strong walls
That kept him always secure
Piercing all life's loveliness
Tapping on a heart's dark door

Seeking the greater gifts
Always desiring more
Yet, ever frequent wonders
Are small, subtle, demure

Drifting in the gentle way
Current, strong and sure
Soaking in the beauty
Find your breeze and soar

An act of gentle kindness
Given from a deepening store
Reflected in the eyes
Love's ever-present cure

Walking Today

Walking today on the path set before me,
I seek the strength to seek the strength of God.
Thoughts arrive, bombard, float by
this busy garden of choice, intent, temptation.

Constantly reminded to slow and to breathe,
Wonder why oft I seek this lesson to relearn.
Remembering to be gentle with a young heart,
give myself permission to question and search.

Taunted and tempted by man and dark imp,
darkness, nudging, subtle, dims the way.
Egos' traps set and avoided, set yet again,
ever-deepening trust in grace lights this day.

Walking today on the paths set before us,
we seek the faith and trust to walk a new step.
We stumble, are made whole in healing.
After distraction, see God's present Light.

Through the Wrath

Moving past the anger
Moving through the wrath
Walking through the fire
Whilst staying on the path

Begging to grant forgiveness
Needing God's great grace
Chest and head are aching
Hot anger on my face

Breathe in each new Breath
Let the pressure go
Longing for the Water
Living in the Flow

Reflections

With renewed aplomb
And heightened suffering
Lessons of one
Arrive always in thirds

Trials of the dark chasms
Held in place by the strings
Web of great bliss
Woven by the forgiven masses

With refreshed desire
Walker walks another day
Looks at the reddening sky
Reflected in her sadness

Stevie Ray Robison

Thankfulness

Thankfulness flows
from the one who remembers;
he walked in the great misery,
the bold suffering of his heart.

Lost then his way,
so many years ago;
saved from his bondage,
he was freed from his self.

Today, he walks in light,
each day brighter than the last;
prays for deeper faith
surrendering the lost past.

The Softer Way

Drama, chaos, exaggeration
The stories that allow
The tellers of those stories
To not see the real life
Arising around them

At all cost
They must protect the need
To protect the delusions
That keep them in safety
The relative safety of the dream

The tellers of story
The keepers of the lies
Touch the unbelievers
Give them something to cling to
Give them something to believe in

People will believe
All they need to believe
To live in the shadow
Of the lies of the dream
It is the way of the soft many

Stevie Ray Robison

Circuitous Meanderings

Circling emotions
Devouring the lost truth
Where did the sanity go?
What is left to lose?

Ignorant refrains
From the monkey or the mouse
Standing in the doorway
Of the rickety old house

Lost in the maze of distrust
Discouraged in each dying day
Though the morning brings always new solace
Trials knock us off the righteous way

Rocky and painful path
Covered in small glowing stones
Tired of the constant growing pain
Weary all the way to our bones

Circuitous meanderings
Of a gawking and salient old sage
Hoping for return of bright hope
And finding the key to his cage

This Moment

With every precious moment
In each of God's new days
Let's see with open eyes
And walk the sacred ways

The glory of His presence
Is here for us to know
When blessings, we receive
In times both high and low

Remembering to thank Him
His gifts flow even more
He wants to see us happy
Let's knock on heaven's door

In every glorious moment
God's peace and love flow free
Let's eat the Bread of Life
Let's live in harmony

Stevie Ray Robison

Final Song's Hopeful Dawn

He learned only today
Two weeks left to live
Cried a hundred tears
Found several unmet fears

Realized as the sun was setting
Half a day wasted
In the misery of loss
As yet unrealized

Rose quickly from his morass
Chose to live in joy and bliss

Treasuring the view
Of the bird on his windowsill

Singing a new song
An everlasting song
In a captured moment

Manners

Expectancies dwell
In the minds of the masses
Manners, mores, beliefs, wonderings
Judged for good
Judged for ill
The simplistic way

To expand beyond
The limits of expectations
Experiential assuredness
Is a frequent wish
Beyond the simplistic
Where judgment wanes

Walking in karma
She nudges and points the way
But the huddled masses
Find comfort behind
The tall row of hedges

Hedging the truth
The mysteries stay frozen
As they dwell within
Judgments, expectations
And manners

Stevie Ray Robison

Washed Away

bitter memories
better horizons
in the mind's unrealized truth
anger rising from the midst of lies
dishonest mysteries stay silent

opening hearts to sights unseen
by eyes closed to the misery
of a world filled in fearful fates
bodies of casualties litter the path
ancient flies filled with malice
suck at the remaining misery
of the wallowing undead

bitter memories
anger flows and burns
from the disingenuous souls
of the wandering masses

bitter memories
spat into the abyss
spat into the timeless void
washed away by choice
washed away by holy blood
washed away for all time
washed away

Universal Truths

Out of the lost silent mysteries of universal truths,
Spring all the answers to all questions asked,
To be caught and known by those who choose,
To open their hands, minds, souls, hearts.

One mind is connected to the wholeness of truth;
All minds are one in this pervasive knowledge;
Opening doors, windows – tearing down barriers,
Mind of the seeker is opened to all truths sought.

All creation exists in the blink of divinity's eye.
The wind carries the songs of forever and never.
Simplicity speaks through the voice of a child,
All colors of the universe in a box of crayons.

So...

Color.
Dance.
Play.
Watch a cartoon.
Make love.
Enjoy a sweet treat.

Whatever you do, do it for that moment.
And do it with all that you are.

Stevie Ray Robison

Be.
Live.
Enjoy.

Moved

i am moved by the sunset
and the sunrise
and the circling hawk

i am moved by the ocean
and the mountain
and the rocky path

i am moved by emotion
love, passion, joy, bliss
and their perfect attainment

i am moved by kindness
committed and true
given without cost, without expectation

i am moved by the forces
of energy pervading all
light, love, nirvana

i am moved by song
and by dance
and by the dancer
committed to the dance

i am moved by the circle

Stevie Ray Robison

life begetting life
love begetting love
karma's unchangeable force
and the changing of that same karma
in the manifesting of miracles

i am moved by the innocent mind
whether infant or ancient
which seeks only to love and be loved

i am moved by creation
the wondrous smile
of one who creates

i am moved when i see a lost one found
opening eyes
opening hearts

i am moved by unselfishness
humbly offering more than expected
with no thought of reward

i am moved by attainment
of our highest purpose
mine, yours, or ours

i am moved by the flow of life
by a universal good
underlying all seen and not

i am moved in the union of two
surrendering all of me
to all of you

i am moved in the feast of life
to taste-smell-touch-see-know
all that life offers
in this perfect moment
and the next

Quiet Suddenness, Return to Grace

Quiet soul floating along
Sea of still and tranquil rest
Riding the waves of foreverness
Finding old peace and new happiness

Startled by the suddenness
Jostled awake by the rising tide
Storm on the horizon
Foreboding awesome dark skies

Crashing thunderous noise
Chaos born of restored fear
Shaken by the vastness
Overwhelmed in the tumultuous surprise

Leaving the faith
In a boat lost in the heights
Crushing waves surround
Dark sky lit by crazed flashes

A moment's thought
Returns them to grace
Riders of the perfect rain
Held safe in the sea of eternity

Choices on the Path

In every living moment
Choices present themselves
Every step, every thought
Each and every perception

A song plays in the hearing
Of a walker on the path
Does the walker pause to listen?
Does the listener stop to dance?

Passing another on the road
Does he turn his head?
Does he greet the other?
Do they exchange a glance? A word?

Yesterday's choices
Presented again today
Risking a change in path
Choosing a new way

Lessons deepen
As time walks on
Higher calling
In each new dawn

Wonders

Basking in the bright morning sun
Warmed in the beauteous Love of God
Perfection in this moment of simplicity
Alive in the wonders of today

Graciously persisting
Gratefully existing
Marvelously wandering
In the wonders of today

Warmed in a lovely new morning
Praising the God of all peace
Walking onward in divinity
Alive in the wonders of today

Chapter 3 – Heaven

Together

Lead me back home
Your Spirit lives in me
Return me to your grace
Your word, it sets me free

Rising yet again
Perfection in this time
Oneness in The Christ
Overwhelmingly divine

Soften now my heart
In this moment, true
Take me back home
Together now with You

Instant of Perfection

Having crossed the threshold
Of the doorway leading to
Mysteries' revelations
Divinity shining through

Having seen your face
Bright, dazzling, and true
Bathed in your light
Child's belief grew

Having stood upon the peak
Breathtaking mountain view
Remembering the walk
That made this one anew

Having found the light
Home where angels flew
Heaven's dawning instant
One in love with you

Flowing Divine

Swimming across divinity's quiet stream
Leaving the shore's earthen solid dream
Drenched in the waters of ever-growing life
Journey of the fallen, departing from strife

Sorrows fade from conscious view
From the swimmers in the waters blue
Warmed by the midday sun of bright
Bathed in the ripples, healed in the light

Joining with all the souls now found
Miracles manifest, no longer bound
Separate no more, joined in holy rain
Alive forever in the sacred song's refrain

All is divine in the acceptance of now
Healing arrives to those who ask how
Surrendering all, God's mind restores peace
Leave now the prison, dive in, find release

To be in God, relinquish all right
Swimming the Waters, cease now the fight
Deepening peace, releasing the mind
Blood of the Christ, flowing, divine

Seek the peace of God's perfect heart

Stevie Ray Robison

Believe and trust; dive, make a start
Risk it all to find the true Face
Live in Love's perfecting embrace

Providence has promised all you desire
Be sanctified now, melded in the fire
Continue to live in the peaceful way
Swim in the waters of Divinity today

A prayer of unity from a humble Son
Thanking His Father for the flowing One
Believe, believe, believe some more
Choose to knock on heaven's great door

Walk, with trust, into Waters Divine
Join now in the One True Mind
In peace, perfected, live now as One
Lovingly abiding in a perfect Rising Sun

Just Beneath

Just beneath the surface
The answers lie in wait
Open to the truth
Approach the hidden gate

Find a piece of life
Revel in its taste
No time like this moment
Come now and make haste

Existing to exist
Is not the chosen place
Of those who've tasted more
And glanced at heaven's face

So, take a look beneath
Find the secret of peace
Gaze into the wisdom
Embrace its great release

Angel's Song

Long flowing hair
Golden as the sounds of her song
Voice that fills the world
And lingers with each note

Radiantly shining
Filling hearts with light mystery
Confident and forever sure
Love is her way

Song of a visiting angel
Flows to the hearts that hear
Visions of loveliness
Spring from each new beat

Heaven's quiet messenger
Delivering divinity's words
Hear them and join the dance
Forever in the perfection of now

Pleased

In this pleasing moment
All peace pervades
With each inward breath
With each smile witnessed

I watch over each soul
Hold every heart in my hands
I am with you all
In the divinity of our embrace

This day, I created
To be cherished by my sons
To be relished by my daughters
To be shared by us all

In this pleasing moment
My peace pervades
With each outward breath
With each smile shared

Stevie Ray Robison

Empty Vessel

Instantaneous revelations
Accepting this moment's grace
Glory's great perfection
Creation's wondrous face

Alive in the dawning shades
Magnificent, colorful sight
Join now in divinity
Creation's wondrous light

Surrendering all that remains
Empty the vessel of love
Prepared for God's great blessings
Delivered by angels above

Deeper

deeper into the heart's song of praise
worship enveloped his wholeness
as he emptied his thoughts, set down his burdens

deeper into the mysteries of the Spirit's presence
songs' words chosen
by the alchemy of synchronous wavelets
divine tapestry woven, worn in glory, woven again

deeper into the secret place of the souls' embrace
Providence welcomed by the glorious song
messengers of Love leading the way
in the words and notes of the music of praise

deeper into the place of oneness
sharing the heart of the songs' soulful leading
angels' presence felt and heard and somehow...
known

ancient prophets' prophecies renewed presence
of one true mind, one true spirit
one true song

deeper into the knowledge of the formless
divine messengers leading the way
leading the song

filling the day

deeper into the song of the accompanists
in joy, in bliss, in soulful calm, in the heart
of beauty

one in the newfound depths
one in the Mind of Providence
one in the angels' new song

Brightened Skies

As eyes look toward the brightening skies,
As a heart moves toward the power of providence,
As thoughts turn to moments to come,
I am filled with the love that is our great gift.

As I move from monotonous days of dim,
As I find the strength within to stand,
Guided to the hopefulness of today,
I am filled with the joy that floods our soul.

As my mind turns to the comfort of trust,
As I choose to walk on in this new day,
As I risk the pain of defeat and fate,
I leap to the place of sacred mighty grace.

As my spirit is stilled in the beauty of calm,
As I fly into ever-brightening skies,
As I walk through the divinity of heaven's gate,
I dwell in the holy heights of one heart's home.

Resting

Resting
> for just a few moments

Basking
> in the midday sun

Feeling
> the sprouting of joy

Living
> in the fellowship of man

Sharing
> the love God has given

Hearing
> the sounds of Creation

Feeling
> the winds of change

Breathing
> the fresh, clean air

Praying
> for God's presence

Believing
> all prayers are answered

Knowing
> God is here

Resting
> in the holy Breath of Love

Chapter 4 – Love

Grace's Invitation

Abundant possibilities
Flow from the warmest hearts
Fire of the ancients
Fuels the blazing desires

Innocent intents
Demanding the greatest gifts
Stored for a time
By the same mind that chose to wake

From the oceans of blessings
On the rising tides of this day
Love is creation's messenger
Deliverer of all

Perfect recognition
From the faith of the contrite
Clearing away obstructions
That took away our sight

Abundant possibilities
Flow from the ready hearts
Into a world of grace
The circle of love complete

Stevie Ray Robison

Love's Message

Breezes of light caress your cheek
You, the one who stands
Alive and in great glory
In the streaming sun of a new day

Gazing at the sky with closed eyes
Imaginings of wondrous calm stillness
Standing naked in Creation's wonder
Field of grains waving with you

Notes of the angels' song
Barely perceptible below the screams of joy
From you, the silent child, basking, loving

The joy fades, replaced by perfect peace
Perception grows; my peace is with you
My love washes over you, embracing you

We enjoy the angels' wondrous song
We live in the perfect glory of this moment
You and me, as One

And you hear me
Accompanied by the messengers of song
Accompanied by their bright melody
I sing to you, "I love you. I love you."

Earthen Beginnings

Earthen beginnings
Ornamental wanderings
Together in certain fate
Two forever joined

Oaths shared in faith
Providence looking on
Persimmon and cinnamon
Fueling the senses

Once and forever
In honor and great truth
Walking rejoinder
Not a moment to lose

Loosed of the bondage
That tied the lost trust
Love flowing freely
Through the river of One

Earthen beginnings
Crockery thrown
Glazed in real beauty
Baked in the fiery kiln

Stevie Ray Robison

Humble Me

Humble me, my God
I am not worthy to see your holy face
Your might is far beyond
All that any could conceive

Humble me, oh God
Burn away my reluctance to surrender
Take all that is within me
That would keep me from you

Humble me, Most High
More fiery than the sun is your gaze
Restore me to the burnt ashes
I am unworthy of the life you give

Take me, oh God
Break my willful spirit
Erase my confident thoughts
Take the humanity from me

Sanctify me, dear God
My soul longs to be cleansed
Destroy my evil essence
Remove my fearful resistance

Purify me, oh great Fire

Melt me down to divinity's core
So all that remains
is the connection to you

Take me, my God
I offer all I am
I long to be cleansed
So that I might be in your presence

Love me, dear God
Let our wills be one
Melt me to the core
Fill me in your love

Stevie Ray Robison

Transformed

Tears streaming through a feigned smile
This shallow water that we wade in tonight

Warm but with chilly undercurrents
Many emotions just beneath a shiny veneer

Weary tiredness from feelings pushed deep
The scream of forever longing to escape

But a prompting of the Spirit renews my mind
And all the blessings of heaven flood my soul

The Holy Mind of God is miraculous power
Healed of all strife, stripped of fear this hour

Sacred Words of God escape from my mouth
Faith wrought hope wrought miraculous love

Basking in the Light, alive in the wondrous sound
Angels surround, lift this wounded child

Newfound Joy

Abounding moments of joy
In the giggle of the children
Living in the memories of each of us
Residing in the place of forever light

Unending feelings of peace
In the knowledge of the perfection
Of the universal plan of love
Of the place of wondrous calm

Tentative glances at the mirror
Into the deep eyes of the sage
Into the innocent eyes of the child
Into the unique beauty that is you

These pervasive thoughts and beliefs
Help us to remain in love's glory
Help us to abide in the wonderment
Of this life of utter and constant bliss

New moments of unending joy
Rising moments of unstoppable love
Glorious moments in creation's light
Alive in the wonder of now with you

Stevie Ray Robison

Inside

Deep within the winding thoughts
There, the truest mysteries hide
Open the sacred chest of old
And risk to look at what's inside

Only love and hope exist
To he who chooses to believe
Miracles, in truth, persist
Manifest what you conceive

Choose this moment now to see
Eyes of love that look at you
Reflected in the mirrored flow
Choose right now to see anew

Let this instant stretch in time
Walk each moment in the truth
Created perfect in perfect love
See the wonder of your youth

Deep within your truest heart
There, the truest mysteries hide
Look at life with God's pure love
And risk to look at what's inside

To Lead

To humbly teach
What we have learned
To share the lessons
Together discerned

A destined work
A gift to give
Open to all
Shining the Light

To teach, to love
To lead the way
Potter's Hands
Molding clay

To humbly share
What we have gained
These gifts of God
Pure hearts sustained

A Hint of New Beginnings

Just over the horizon
We can sense the aroma
Of the fresh spring flowers
Contemplating their birth
Deep in the still frozen ground

Just out of earshot
The song of the bluebird
Reaches our hearts
As we listen
In humble faith

Just around the next bend
Hope stands strong
For two who seek
Both the mind and the heart
Of a God of Perfect Love

Just beyond what we
Can see and hear and sense
There is the place
Where miracles are born
And healing awaits

Living in the Midst

From the midst of the silent song
Between the notes with no sound
There, exists the real peace
Waiting forever to be found

Where love and passion merge
Excited in the creation of glee
Dance and play in this instant
Revel in the great mystery

Alive in the neverending bliss
Joyous in the sanctity of life
Released in fires of cleansing
No longer holding fear or strife

In the midst of the neverending song
We dance and sing in true love
Serenaded by scores of God's angels
Divinity arrives from above

Stevie Ray Robison

Emigrant

He arrived from a distant land
Where homes were made of snow
Seeking a breadth of experience
In the valley far below

Trudging down the slope
For all of three long weeks
He wept most every morning
As the sun rose o'er the peaks

An old life left behind
A new life just ahead
He wanted to turn back home
But kept on the path instead

A thousand drifting thoughts
He caught and left on the way
Along with the extra coats
Leaving each and every day

So, when he arrived in the valley
Lighter of clothe and of mind
He'd left all he was on the mountain
Journeyed straight through the divine

Now, he walks through the towns every evening

Helping lost souls when he can
Sometimes mistook for an angel
Though by his own words, he's a man

He never discusses religion
Though acquainted with beings, divine
He believes it best for each journeyer
To seek and discover each sign

He's walked every night for millennia
And finally, it's time to depart
Carrying the burdens of millions
Mountains await his worn heart

The trek to his home will be harsh
As each step enlarges his peace
He knows that the peaks hold the secret
That home is the place of release

Dark times in humanity's valley
Will linger until his return
A few hundred decades of sorrows
Whose reason no man can discern

But this is the way it must be
As even a Buddha needs rest
Let's pray that his time will return
And for strength to walk on through this test

Stevie Ray Robison

Glorious Love

For the first time in her life,
she stood unsure
of what tomorrow would bring.
She finally chose
the noble path of surrender,
dove into the abyss,
releasing
her desires and beliefs
as she entered
the empty nothingness
of eternal bliss.

To know is not to live;
life is indeed to be lived.
Expectancy squelches
the harmonious yet invisible ripples
of creation's waking tides.
She realized and acknowledged
that she was not the wave,
not the ebb nor the flow.

She reveled
in the emptiness
of Glorious and Divine Love.

Pursuit

I'll chase you in the morning
Pursue you every day
My love grows stronger with each word
In all I hear you say

The arrows of my love
Are flaming in desire
Soaring through the air
Consumed in holy fire

Forever, I will follow
My everlasting flight
Soaring in your glory
Made new in heaven's sight

I'll chase you in this instant
And every instant hence
Forever, I will follow
Forever, I will run

Chapter 5 – One

Charisma

Awakened in the shining moment
When strength meets calm resolve
Man finds his place in the world
Holding Charisma in his open hand

Deep within his humbled heart
He surrenders to find real peace
Mighty warrior's ancient truth
Spirit of Light displaces fear

Touched by the mighty Hand of God
Alive in the kind wonderment of unity
Seeking the bosom of compassion
Unified circle - man, woman, God

Stevie Ray Robison

Peaceful Moment's Knowing

Water ever flowing
Shimmers in the light
Ancient gift of knowing
Streams of perfect sight

Feel the rippling breeze
Taste the flowing air
Curing all unease
Ending all despair

Take a moment's rest
Leave the cares behind
Rising from the west
Feel the wind, divine

Glory rising now
Release the waning need
Harvest is forever
To they that plant the seed

Peaceful water flowing
Shimmering in the sun
Ancient gift of knowing
Rest in the peace of One

One Heart

Seeking love and bliss
With a heart of faithful trust
Love and bliss
Are surely received

Seeking joy and glee
With a heart of love and bliss
Joy and glee
Are surely received

Seeking the one true light
With a heart of joy and glee
The one true heart
Is found

Stevie Ray Robison

They Smiled

Father within
Looks at His son
Son in the house
Looks to the One

Father above
With adoration, much
Great Hand reaches
Son feels the touch

Father pervades
All He has made
Hears the request
Son has just prayed

Father of all
Son of all, too
Connected, as one
Divine through and through

Son's Holy Father
Father's true Son
Power and Love
Flowing as One

Son and the Father

One and the same
Living this moment
From sacred place came

He watches His Father
And watches His Child
Together and separate
In this moment smiled

Stevie Ray Robison

As One

As one, we walk this holy day
Forever together, come what may
Your mercy shines from each bright face
Alive in your divine embrace

Sacred wonders touch each heart
May fear and suffering now depart
Soaked in your magnificent rain
We sing with angels this holy refrain

Glory streams from your heavenly love
Joined in song by angels above
As one, we sing this sacred day
Grateful for you, in all we say

As one, we're healed by your great hand
Together in unity, forever we stand
Your holy word fills all the land
Each ray of light, each grain of sand

Your sacred wonders touch each life
Of we who walk through trial and strife
The price of grace paid by the Son
We stand in unity, joined as one

Sacred Connected Whole

Very deep within me
I feel the wonder of your presence
We are alive in perfect oneness
Sacred connected whole

Brother of forever
Let me feel your healing light
Let me bask in wondrous love
Sacred connected whole

Flood me in your peace
Teach me in your ways
Friend to all mankind
Sacred connected whole

Divinity rising within
Christ alive in me
Let us share your healing ways
Sacred connected whole

Holy Unity

Moving beyond the present space
Leave the cares of this world for a time
Breathe deeply in the healing air
We remind ourselves it isn't there

Moving beyond what senses sense
One true peace, there to be met
Vibrations beyond the flowing waves
Here is where we truly touch

Moving beyond perceptions of time
Be merged in the true Mind of God
Breathe the divinity of unity
Healed in one true thought

Return Again

From the ashes,
>I have risen,
>>watered by your living love.

From the burnt wasteland
>of so many yesterdays,
>>I find the hope
>>>in your constant bright light.

Return me to pure darkness,
>burn me to the core;
>>fill me with your holy fire,
>>>cleanse me in your terrible ire.

The wickedness of youth –
>lead me back to there.

Fill my heart with misery,
>flood me in despair.

Return to me, oh God.

Return me, too, to you –
>extinguished in the waters of life,
>>rising once again.

Here and Now

God
Alive and present
Source
Flowing and forever
Creator
A universe for you
Connection
Way of truth in light
Helper
Guardian on the path
Lover
Passionately moving your heart
Savior
Hope for all eternity
Teacher
Showing the way to peace
Father
Speaking to His son
Brother
Showing the way to One

God is good
God is alive
God is pervasive
God is present
God is forever

God is truth
God is light
God is love
God is One
God is without
God is within
God is conscious
God is your every waking thought
God is the flow of the dream
God is here
God is now

Feel Him
Touch Him
Connect with Him
Be in Him
Be One in God
Here and Now
Be One in God

Stevie Ray Robison

Seven Rungs on the Ladder of Love

If peace and harmony
Are truly the aim
We must be willing
To discard the same
Climb the ladder
Higher each day
Walk in grace
Live in the Way

In forgiveness and kindness
Lifting tall
Climbing higher
Appreciate all
Willing to leave
The lower rungs
For the good of all
For the good of One

Revulsion
Animosity
Distaste
Neutrality
Attraction
Devotion
One

Stevie Ray Robison

Chapter 6 - Leap

All

Changing constants
A world renewed with each blink
Fading of insanities
As dusk settles on old truth

Join the newly Conscious
Dive into Nirvana's crux
Awakening spirits arising
In the falling of old beliefs

Set all the past to rest
And head for Saturn's rings
Joining in the splendor
The party's just begun

Follow not the leaders
But lead the followers new
Painting a wondrous rainbow
In colors never seen

Clear the ancient wreckage
It wreaks of old remains
Nothing left to salvage
The changing of refrains

Choose the dawning sprinkles

Of one collected rain
Cleansing all illusion
Till naught remains the same

The time to come is now
Collaborations call
Leave the old behind
And join the newfound All

Glory, Divine

Leap into forgiveness
Be enlivened in perfect love
Find the grace of this instant
Revel in my glory, divine

The speed of your thoughts
Will carry you to safety
In the slightest instant
You are saved by my grace

Lift your eyes to the sky
Let me take your heart in mine
Be enlightened in an instant
Abide in my glory, divine

Stevie Ray Robison

Emerge

Far off in the unseen distance
Saxophone plays its lonesome song
Listeners in the darkness
Huddled masses lost for a time

Dreamer weaves a midnight dream
All the threads connected
In a tapestry of life
Hope is resurrected

Home in an instant's ride
Colors of all nature
And others beyond
The great divide approaches

Beaming in the wonders
Of life beyond all life
Diving into splendors
Beyond the simple sight

Just beyond the darkest place
Abysmal wonders showing true
Know that home is waiting there
Emerge renewed and be at One

Quiet Walk

Quiet walk on the subtle deer path
Shaded by the ancient giants
Gazing deeply into the silence
Starting anew on the contrite journey
Fears dissipate on the rays
Through the small holes in the covering
Streaming from the heavens above
Unseen in this instant, yet always there
God of foreverness here in this moment
Subtly touching this subtle child
Barely perceivable yet overwhelming flood

Songs of angels accompany the walk
Deeply moving the waiting quiet soul
Raging calm tides move the still
Inviting the inferno of utter divinity
Return to the holy ashes of creation
Sparked by a humble and quiet prayer
Sparked by a contrite and needy soul

Invited by this unworthy child
Accepted by this lover of God
Touched by God's own hand
Healed in the salvation of this instant
Changed forever in the bathing of Love
Changed forever in the perfection of God

Stevie Ray Robison

Praising now and forever this gift
Salvation here in a holy instant
Perfection dawns in a humble prayer
Returning to Creation's Divine Hand

A Single Tear

A single tear is the dam
That holds back a mighty flowing river
Such suffering surrounds us today
Such misery in the hearts of those we pass

In the dawning instant of true love
A butterfly floats by with grace
Reminds us of the hope that surrounds
The spark in the hearts of those we pass

> *Dear God,*
>
> *Set free the flood*
>
> *Give us the grace*
> *To ask for the strength*
> *To take the true risk*
> *To surrender to you*
> *To choose to allow*
> *Your perfect love*
> *To heal all the world*
>
> *Beginning*
>
> *With a single tear*

Amen

A single tear is the dam
That holds back a mighty flowing river
All spiritual gifts are at your command
All we ask is ours
All we desire is stored up for us

Waiting

For an instant of change
For an instant of love
For a single tear
That sets free a river

The river of divine and perfect love
The flowing river of your healing
The source of miracles
Let it be so

And so it is

Genuine Perfection

Genuinely human
Perfectly divine
Living in truth
Brilliantly shine

Lover of life
Each wondrous day
Walking in wakefulness
Follows the way

Attracting great gifts
Highest mind's will
Courageous in faith
Peaceably still

A life of no limits
Choose to believe
Creator of thoughts
Bound to achieve

Lover of life
This and each day
Attractor of goodness
In joy, always stay

Dark Corners

From the darkest corners of misery
Grow the subtle agents of change
In the dimly lit lost memories
Clever, dark, and strange

There crosses the angel of dark
With wings of gold and steel
Touching the ancient fearfulness
Painted with the mystical seal

Enlivened in the state of pain
The walker walks the path
Dying in mysterious losses
Crippled by the unending wrath

From the darkest corners of fear
From a mind of chaos and loss
He clings to life's old lessons
No matter what the cost

But light springs from the depths
With a choice to see and do
The glory of the dreams
That flow through life renewed

Alloy

Holy Fires
Burn me to the core
Stream of Love
Take the final thoughts

In Oneness and grace
Melted in the flames
Forever in peace
Lost in the elemental place

Perfect passion
Soothe my aching heart
Diving into
Infinite cavernous black

Kissed by the ripples
Caught up in the Flow
Well of all divinity
Feeding Creation's one

Spring of Ecstasy
Quench the unquenchable thirst
Restore a lost soul
Returning to the breeze

The candle's flame burns
Ego's waning wick
Dancing in Divinity's breeze
Epiphanous song of Love

Holy Fires
Melting in the cauldron
Melding into perfection
One true Alloy

Reawakened

He was recreated by the great creator
Abiding within his contrite and softened heart
Flew among the soaring hawks
Sang the ancient lessons of angels' flowing art

Awakened in the quiet awakening
Storms moved his soul to truly change
Sought solace in the winds of forever
And wisdom in the healing rains

Wandered quite far from the path
Yet, the changed man still exists
As he walks into the tempering blaze
He grasps that love persists

A time of great renewal
Greets his softened heart
Come feast upon his magic
Enjoy his heartfelt art

Ancient Surrender

Oh Fires of the Ancient Dance
Tempt me in your passion
Drive me to unknown wonders
In the ecstasy of your Heat

Awakening slowly from sleep
The drifter wanders to the edge
Abysmal views, dark and hidden
Walks into the weightless depths

Oh Fires of the Blooming Rose
Stimulate my every raw sense
Aroma-filled mysteries of love
Seduce my rippling thoughts

Limitless colorful plummet
Old thoughts rising from sleep
Walker descends in silence
Great glories fading from view

Oh Fires of Exploding Magma
Join me in a secret embrace
Ecstasy dawns in our screams
Devoid of the empty truths

In a perfect instant of peace

The Glory of Light flashes forth
Journey of the colorful walker
Ends in a merging of Love

Oh Fires of Cold Insanity
Relieve this once proffered need
Dive now into my openness
We'll merge in a moment untold

Chapter 7 – Revelation

Mystic Truths

Old is new
And new is old
Where time is timeless
And truth unfolds

Sacred moments
Are always near
In view of love
Devoid of fear

Mystic truths
Are simply known
To open eyes
They're always shown

So wake from sleep
Enjoy the ride
And bathe in light
From deep inside

Useful Quest

The beauty of life
Changing, ebbing, flowing
Can never be
Fully understood

The usefulness of life
Found
In the constant quest
For its usefulness

Once found
The quest ends
The destination reached
The usefulness ends

It is thus better
More peaceful and kind
To not be obsessed
In the quest to find
The totality of usefulness

New Century

Black century comes to its fateful end
Age of great turmoil and suffering
Plague of locusts and leaf and mud
Grasshopper springs into the new year

Purple and yellow flowers explode
As the season of change starts new
Time's clock watched by the ten
Holding the universal change at bay

Forever began with a bold wink
From the young whippoorwill's song
Bright and hopeful, looming large
Century of wisdom began with a wane

Moon is bright again this bold night
Magic settles in for the common folk
Mysteries solved by the rising mystic
Book of secrets told to one and all

The Three Voices

Chaotic dreams of the psychotic darkness
spill into this bright and beautiful new day.
"Why are there so many conflicting thoughts
and desires? Why can't I make them go away?"

"Peace is in the eternal Mind of God." I hear
myself with such wisdom and conviction. Yet
another voice, clear and present, also beckons
me thus "I need to be heard. I need to be
loved. I need to be filled. I need to understand."
These needs, these requests, these demands,
seemingly reasonable and innocent, are the
reason for my lapses of peace.

"Show me the light of true wisdom, Father."
I hear, unsure, which of the two voices
this time is speaking. Perhaps, on the other
thought, it is another voice. Three voices,
three conflicting sets of wants and needs.
The child needs; the Self knows; the negotiator
tries to make sense of it all.

> *"The negotiator has the final say. The
> negotiator is the home of free will. Choose
> well and with much care. Hear the others,
> yes, and then, choose well."*

He Knew

He knew the tastes
Of chocolate and cherries
Of divinity and fate
Of yesterday and today

He knew the uniqueness
Of majestic sunsets
Sunrises, eclipses
Even the darkest nights

He knew he was touched
By God's own great hand
He knew the beauties
Of gratitude and peace

But mostly he knew
How to be just as he was
And to be content
In the serenity of acceptance

Stevie Ray Robison

Quest for Peace

For uncountable lifetimes
He sought all manner of things
Riches, romance, fame, fulfillment
Never content, never resting

He had been a traveling musician
A sharecropper earning his keep
Once he had been a prince
He died in a quest for more lands

So many wonderful and wondrous lives
He was forever a part of the seams of life
Forever sunk into a sea of want
Forever ensnared in the unquenchable quest

For uncounted lives
His story many times told
Until at last he was awakened
By the horrid siren
Of the lust for more

And he found rest
At last

Birthing Creation's Power

Where dreams are given form
From the birthplace of emotions
The soul is fed
In the wonders of experience

The true and final moments
Rise on the quantum waves
And life is given truth
In the glory of a thought

Thoughts are made manifest
To feed the soul
With the nutrients of feelings
Purposing this realm

Where dreams are given form
From the cradle of the universe
One with God's true mind
The soul is given life

Grief's Abandonment

Floating through the soundless vacuum
Of the blackest blackness of space
Twinkling hope fades
Replaced by the loss of all

She once walked in majesty
Alive in the hope of tomorrow
But all her dreams shattered
With the beating of the final drum

Floating through the mysteries
Of a hint of fresh white blossoms
The trees of her forever loss
Still find reason to be renewed

Grief persists for a time
Until she chooses to set it down
Lays the burned carcasses
In the high grasses adjacent to life's path

As she walks away from grief's load
Left safe in its new home
Her eyes are free to gaze
At the dawning beauties of spring

Passing the trees again

She stops this time to enjoy
The fresh blossoms of new life
Places just one
Securely in her pocket

Floating through the soundless choices
In the vagaries of varying decisions
She smiles as she realizes
She left her regrets in the grasses
Secured with her abandoned grief

Stevie Ray Robison

Manifest Gratitude

Aligned in deep gratitude
With the Creator of all
As wills, human and divine, merge
Blessings flow freely

Whether unseen or seen
Unacknowledged or acknowledged
Providence actualizes all matter
Creates all that will ever be

Limits are formed only in the mind of fear
Belief, in grateful joy, removes all limits
With mind, heart, soul in tune with Love
Infinity creates all that is imagined

Replace

Replace...

Fear with courageous love
Anger with patient acceptance
Disappointment with utter faith
Lack with great abundance
Chaos with alignment
Drama with ease
Discontentment with gratitude
Suffering with health
Pain with peace
Darkness with light
Blindness with sight
Limits with life

Replace...

Stevie Ray Robison

Life Flows

When time had no meaning
There was no time
Just before it dawned
It was hidden from the mind of all
Energy existed only as potential
In the timeless Mind of Creation
And in less than an instant
Creation created a universe
And in that universe
Was time and space and energy
A place we could find a home
A place where thought could become form
A place where love could mold matter
A place where life could be perpetuated
Life that was and is self-aware and self-sustaining
Life multiplied and multiplies still
Life flows, in time, through time, harmonious, true
Life flows on

The Cluttered Closet

The dream persists
As echoes of visions
Shown on the surface
Of the stream of memories
Reviewed for a time
And then either released
Or stored away
And carried

The stored visions of memories
Grow heavier with each day
Fill the closest of our minds
With needless and worthless junk

The dream flows away
From the mind that chooses
To release the need
To remember the present
And store it away
In that cluttered room
Of the cluttered mind

The dream flows away
From the one who surrenders
The need to place value
On all those items

Stevie Ray Robison

Stored in the closet

Close the door to the closet
Live in this instant
And be free
Be free

Perfect Mindfulness

Looking at the possibilities of today
Perspectives float before the mind
Each new choice spurns yet another
All leading to the same destined end

Tomorrow's perfection is assured
In the mind of a hopeful dreamer
Creative thoughts rise from this moment
Form the path the follower follows

Looking back to the lessons once learned
Following the thoughts that led to peace
Choosing that mind that sowed love
Future's perfection is indeed assured

Stevie Ray Robison

Return

Return to the wonderful moment
When love was all you knew
Alive in jubilant glory
Praising all that is true

Love and light and joy
Surrounding an innocent child
Spinning and dancing in fire
In each new moment we smiled

Return to a place of peace
Salvation's ever-flowing way
Rejoicing in Love's forever
Each moment of each new day

Salvation is for the living
So take a gulp of life!
Release your insecurities
Your fears, attachments, and strife

Return to your salvation
The moment of love is here
Remember the vision of Peace
In faith, Love will appear

Fruit and Seed

In the merging of peaceful wills
An optimal destiny moves through the great circle
Life finds the true nature of miraculous love
Love finds a way home to the present perception

Each difference between noble will and free will
Creates disturbance in the holy flow of miracles
Realizing oneness in wills and loving flow
The perfection of Divine Merging attained

Distracting thoughts interrupt the great flow
Not of the Divinely Merged Perfection
Not present in the will of the Creator
Are not harmonious with the perfect love

Knowledge and judgment are purveyors of pain
Release these thoughts and merge with Love

Love and joy are the way of the noble child
Be merged in the one true moment of conception

Be glad in the pleasing flow of Divine Source
Gentle joy is the seed and fruit of love's awareness

Chapter 8 – Into the Light

Gloriously Reawakened

The furthest flung mysteries
Come again into view
As the sage reawakens
And sees through eyes, open

Amazing possibilities
Manifest in a thought
Seeking only love
He finds what is sought

Glorious beauty
So strong and alive
Rejoining together
For a glorious ride

New Arrivals

With each dawning day
Brave and bold new arrivals
Fill the landscape of possibilities
To one with eyes open

Let us look to the bright heavens
Pray to the Maker of all
Live in hope for blessings, great
Satisfied by the falling manna

Yesterday's perilous rapids
Waterfalls of treacherous fear
Are but distant memories
As we drift in the wide river

This valley of awakening
Filled by a rising sun
Heals the weary souls
Where God, in Light, is found

Thy Kingdom Come

For just a few moments
She wandered the dark
Lost and alone
Cold, scared, and stark

But then he remembered
And opened his eyes
Was filled with delight
In the glorious surprise

Streams of white light
And every color seen
Shiny and bright
In the glorious sheen

Thy Kingdom Come
Was her solemn prayer
They opened new eyes
And saw God was there

Stevie Ray Robison

Red, Violet, Indigo

Just beyond the limits of periphery
Catch a glimpse of the colors of flow
Red, violet, indigo...
and colors that no one knows

Closing eyes, tight and sure
The warmth of the colors come into view
Red, violet, indigo...
and colors rising anew

Welcome to the dawning realms
Where glory and peace ever dwell
Red, violet, indigo...
and colors no eye can tell

Just beyond the limits of thought
Reach out and touch the bright glow
Red, violet, indigo...
new colors we'll forever know

Life Moves On

To be a droplet of water
in the constant fountain of life
to flow in the natural eternity
is where all glory dwells

Rapid waters, white with rage
merging in the nearest age
tempt the child, confuse the sage
release the tiger from his cage

As the past rushes forward
so the present rushes on
caught in the tremulous stream
caught in a dawning scream

and as the sun sets yet again
on this crazed and wild day
and the moon rushes forth
as the droplets join the flow

life moves on
this moment and the next
water moves forever
through this, the perfect dream

Unbending the Light

Bliss, joy, ecstasy
Kindness, compassion, love
Faith, trust, and hope
All gifts of God above

Anger, fear, lack
Impatience, judgment, greed
Pride, lust, and doubt
Grow from the dark one's seed

The light that is within
Shines through those with sight
Felt by those without
Nature of God's own might

Originates in true perfection
God's most holy light
Filtered by the darkness
Emotions' dampening plight

As a prism bends white light
Dark feelings bend the Glow
Blissful walker is pure and clear
Grace of Spirit purifies the Flow

Angel

He dove into the pool of bliss
Encouraged by the voice of his angel
A night of new wonders
Great mysteries of love revealed

He dove into the ocean of change
Swam through unmeasured time
Dove into the depths of awareness
Accompanied by his angel's glory

He dove into the waves of love
Flew into the forgotten realms
Accompanied forever by a new companion
Encouraged by his angel's voice

He dove into his angel's heart
Forever, they'd live as one
The glory of heaven's true message
Merged in the gift of love

Stevie Ray Robison

Beneath the Surface

She prepared for several moments,
To leave the binding constraints of physics;
Focused on the space in her vision,
Where objects move from solid to blur.

Traveler on the timeless, windless winds,
Beckoned by the music between the notes,
She allowed her cares to drop out of view,
Sought the place from whence she arose.

Closing her eyes, opening her awareness,
Colorless slivers of light just outside her view,
She felt a wave of weariness pass through her,
Disappearing into the pervasive slivers of glow.

Instantly invigorated by the rising strength,
Of the fire ever-burning within her core,
No longer bound by the fleeting thoughts,
She was freed from the departing sensations.

She kindled the eternal fire with her dreams,
Let expectations rise with the smoke and ash;
All that bound her was flowing gently away,
She was ready to begin the ancient dance.

Calm, pleasing, exciting, enticing, freeing,

Spirit of the rhythm moved her to join the beat;
Standing to her feet in the place of her mind,
Witnessed the enchantress become the enchanted.

Entranced in the slices between the sacred beats,
Light mixing with sound, filling her every breath,
She moved without effort, merged with the song:
The song of infinity underlying this lost realm.

Uttering words inaudibly, she listened to the wind;
Babbling in clarity, somehow understanding,
Danced without motion, spoke without sounds,
Finding the peace of divinity's sacred nest.

Time and sound and feelings had drifted away;
She enjoyed the lasting moment of timeless joy,
Lost and found in the sacred, wondrous, bliss,
Awakened in the beat of the song of true peace.

Stevie Ray Robison

The Lost Secrets

We see and hear and touch
Things entering perception
But what, we wonder, lies beneath?
What is the nature of that which moves the heart?

The mythical mystic behind the red curtain giggles
He knows not that he is mere myth
He knows not the limits imposed
By the perception of the imperceptive
He feels not constrained
By the thoughts of the thinking mind

In our deeper mind's ear
We hear the odd sound
The giggling stream of light
The gurgling river of life
The light and sound beneath perception

We ask him
The mystic
Giggling and gurgling
Odd, but knowing

We ask...

And this is what we hear...

The power of touch
Is granted to all
No consequence
Whether old or still small

The power to feel
Is chosen by most
Who stop trying to drive
To breathe in and coast

The power of quiet
Is found by a few
Restoring perfection
As old becomes new

The power of mystery
The other side of peace
Opens new eyes
When sight finds release

The power of truth
That light pervades all
Expansion of energy
The rippling fall

The power of love
Moves every mind
From a world made of matter
To another, new, divine

Stevie Ray Robison

Beneath all these mysteries
(Above if you prefer)
Lies the real power of all
Taste it - you'll concur

The power of the mystic
Hidden in a clear place
Open your heart, your eyes
Brave the lost embrace

Dive into perfection
And all will become real
I dare you now to join me
Let not your thoughts congeal

We wake from the dream, rub the sleep from new eyes. And somewhere in the distance, somewhere inside the walls, we hear a light and tasty giggle...

Child of Perfection

Born in perfection
From an environment of peace
Thrust into a world
Of fears and sorrows

Fear is the father of vice
Sorrow, the mother of loss
In the absence of both
The child lives in perfection

Seek perfection
In this and every moment
Exist not in vice nor loss
But instead,
In comfort and abundance
For there is the Grace of Love

Synergistic

and in your holy presence
synergistic bodies collide
crimson skies upon us
reflecting the burning eyes

his presence leaves the marks
but the wounds no longer bleed
the sacred fires purge
providing all you need

flight of ancient wonders
phoenix finds the source
filled in effervescence
nirvana's newfound course

Sharing the Dream

He rode the waves of blissful destiny
Tossed by the currents rising
Touching, tasting, feeling, sharing
Words of a heart bruised and real

He captured the hearts of a few
Tossed by his rising tides
Leaving small marks on wandering souls
Leaving dark chasms in his lost mind

Oneness with the waves
Tossed by life's lessons
Drenched in the turmoil
Quenched in the flow

Rising above the sea of endlessness
He rides the waves of the sky
Watching and knowing a million hearts
Sharing the songs of life and truth

Stevie Ray Robison

Creation's Frantic Dance

Tell to me your secrets
Reveal the whisperings on a soft wind
Touch me with the light
Of a blazing hot summer sun

I am alive in your presence
I am one in your holy home
Alive in this instant
Joined in divinity's song

Lead me ever deeper
Show me the way that pervades
Take me to the waters' edges
Let me dive into your love

Drench me in the mysteries
Quench me in your infinite ways
Flood my essence with yours
Pull me deeper within

I am alive in your presence
I am one in your holy home
Alive in this instant
Joined in divinity's song

Refresh my aching need

Burn me ever deeper in desire
Overwhelm me in your passion
Lead me in your frantic dance

Feast on this offering
Of a humble, unworthy child
Let your mighty hunger grow
Devour me, make us one

I am alive in your presence
I am one in your holy home
Alive in this instant
Joined in divinity's song

Chapter 9 – Beyond

Unforetold

The infamy of a gift
Contrite walker in awareness
Streaming in the rivers
Of enlightenment's glowing flame

Candle of true love
Burns forever in the thoughts
Holy scribe tells the story
Of enlightenment's glowing flame

Bursting in the ancient colors
Breathing the sacred imaginings
The first dreamers dreamt
Precursor to all existence

Permanence of wonder
Feeding the insatiable quest
Storyteller's walk
In enlightenment's glowing flame

Stevie Ray Robison

Peace, Love, Nirvana

I once met a friend
Whose wishes
Always came true

She taught me the secrets
Of faith and truth
Of manifest perfection
Of utter divinity

The profane had no meaning
Lack, loss, despair, fear
Fell away
Overwhelmed by the bright joy
In the eye of each beholden

I once met a friend
Spent a season in the wash
Of the light
Of peace, love, nirvana

Today
I seek to be
That friend
I once knew

Essence of Grief

I have a heart of forgiveness
I have learned this harsh lesson
Through tearful surrender
Through joyful animosity
Through cherished revenge

I have a heart of charity
Giving until it hurts
Then giving some more
Masochistic longings
To heal all but me

I have a heart for grieving
For grieving my losses
And the losses of all others
Taking away their pain
In forgiveness, charity, grief

Stevie Ray Robison

Parallels

Parallel worlds
Just around
The next waiting bend
Come and explore
The mirror
The rabbit hole
The dark night of the dark mind

Parallel thoughts
Just through
The next feeling
The following sensation
Come and explore
The mystery
The dark chasm
The schism of the dark mind

Parallel souls
Just beyond
The waiting mystery
Wake and explore
Dive into the wonder
Of the dark night of rain
Of the dark reflections of pain
Of the mirror of the dark mind

Parallel visions
Just beyond
The opening eyes
Come and gaze
Into the dark magic
Blue-green eyes
Mirror of strange nearby realms

Sacred Meditation of Ecstasy

Preparing for the moment
When I will see your face
Bright, shining, potent, perfect, divine
Overwhelmed as anticipation builds

Recalling many lessons
Readying for the great instant
I will be caught in your flames
Mere breathing labored
As I continue to prepare
Mind, body, spirit, flame, one

Dismissing all thoughts
But the perfect thoughts of you
Help me to be pure
Empty now my mind

Releasing the power
Into the great earth
She shudders with the impact
Of a humble mystic's strength

Feeling the feelings
As rain drops on my skin
Soaking in
Falling away

Sensations grow stronger
As the fire builds inside
And nature moves and sings
More vibrant than before

More and more empty
Thoughts, feelings, beliefs, sensations
Rolling off my skin
As the raindrops
Fall to earth

Closing my eyes
I see a river of silver
Quicksilver flowing, in oneness

Diving into its divinity
I am quicksilver, too
One with the flow
One in perfection

Opening my eyes
Fire burns all around
Springing from a kindled heart
One with the Flame of Creation

Melt me!
Burn me!
Let us dance the sacred dance...

Stevie Ray Robison

Take me!
Fill me!
Caught up in the trance...

And in this perfect instant
All is one
All is empty
All is flowing
All is alive
All is connected
All is you
All is me

And so it is.
Amen

Falling

A life, filled with fallen dreams
As so many stars in a winter sky
Falling dark midnight of a darker mind

A star descends with each thought
Diving into the abysmal morass
Of humble creation

The moments invade
The quiet pool
Meditation broken

Ripples spread, expansive new realities
Branching forth
Exploding
In the colors of a colorful mind

All that can be seen
Is seen in the dark ancients' thoughts
Cavernous hollows of glory's understatement
Lifting the pensive restful wanderers
Into the service of the One dawning Truth
Into the service of the Wonders of Love
Alive and well in the glimmers
Of a billion watching stars
Each waiting

Stevie Ray Robison

For his chance to serve
For his moment to fall
For his call to descend
Into the perfection
Of the One Waiting Heart

One Waiting Heart
Awakening from a dream
Of stars
Filling the midnight sky
Falling
Glimmering
Streaming
Rippling
Alive

In the Holy Service of Love

Time's Creative Moment

The gray dimness of yesterday's misery
Is fading into the glossy black evil
Pure and void, lost in realms undiscovered
Led by the devious servants of death

Awakening to the dark and winding rhythms
Child remembers the moment when all was dark
Just before the dawning of time
Just before the birth of time's new reality

The child remembers, in the deepest crevices
In the part of the mind only accessible
Freed from past burdens, future worries
The childlike mind has a hint of thought
Of the earliest creative forces
Of the birth of colors, scents, tastes, thoughts
Of the dawning of time
Of the burgeoning of life

Stevie Ray Robison

Beyond a Moment

Just beyond the furthest reaches
Of limited understandings
There is the silent song
Of the wounded rabbit

Just beyond the sunlight
That streams forever true
Just beyond the magic
There, we bid farewell

A moment's ecstasy dawns
As the lovers' music fades
Here in the brokenness
Of a morning's new blossoms

Breathing in the sadness
Breathing out the pain
Walking ever true
In a moment that never ends

Intersecting

Where infinity meets the human mind
There the stark reality of unseen thoughts prevails
Time and space folding into oblivion
A glance at the eternal corners of creation's origin

Finding rest in a peaceful moment of bliss
The walker on the path of discovery peers anew
Curiosity piqued by the dark undergrowth
Of a moment's journey through forever's portal

Where infinity meets the human mind
Divine thoughts of perfection gnaw at the seams
Awakened by the destruction of the final misery
Peacefully existing with all there is

Stevie Ray Robison

Dark Skies

Peruvian dove owns the midnight sky
Black as the black of empty space
Singing the song that can't be heard
Taking the sorrows never displaced

Increasing resignation expands
Purples and greens paint the feral hare
Leaping red mites tear at the flesh
Divining the wonders of the winnowing air

Blood drips warm to the threshing floor
The wheat and the chaff, inseparable loss
Heavy red coat hides the old girth
Obscuring through centuries a once sacred birth

The fight of the ages begins fresh and new
Divine or profane, true love versus fear
Touching another, another draws close
Centuries of voices, once silent, now hear

The star-filled skies offer glimpses of hope
As the angels of death return for their gift
Child of awakening lost in the mist
Opened the seams, tore a fresh rift

Retreating

i began to write a poem
about neverending sadness
pouring down
from the dark skies of impeditive dreams
composed in the instants
of the raining hearts of shameful loss
from the impetuous child, refusing to die

white hot forgiveness from shadows of doubt
refracted from the hours of nagging doom
but into the mirror i braved a gaze
and in in the next holy instant all was changed
reflected in the shining eyes
of you

remaining illusions drained in a beat
of a holy heartbeat filled with fresh meat
karmic, carnal, disturbed, destruction
till all that remains
is all that now matters
shattered
in a moment
of crazed indifference
of dawning forevers
of blazing desire
of new love's touch

Stevie Ray Robison

i began to write a poem
about the dawning of time
and the manifest wonders
of imperfect vision
and the ebbing surrenders
of the towers of dread
where dreams
sometimes fade
but never
end

Dark Silence

silent in the dark

grounded
  for a time
  as his wings
  heal

angels surround
  the chosen one
  healing light
    covers the landscape
  floods his heart

in the wonder of grace
  he does not roam far
    from the perfection
    of his divine truth

stifled in the walk
  for but a moment in time.

...
...

Stevie Ray Robison

silent in the dark

he breathes in the love of God
he reflects on the mirror of Love
he revels in the crucible of One

and he smiles
  at the hope in his heart
  as he remembers

the Holy Dance
  that shall never end...

after just a moment's rest
  (after an eternity's pain)
  carried away
  (on angels' wings)

after but a moment

joy returns
 hope presides
  love congeals
   life flows on...

as he returns
 to the perfect truth
   of the pervasiveness
 of One Eternal Love

For information on other works published by Stevie Ray Robison:

www.livingthepoem.com
www.empoweredbydivine.com

Or on various social networking sites:

facebook.com/livingthepoem
twitter.com/livingthepoem
youtube.com/livingthepoem
reverbnation.com/livingthepoem

Made in the USA
Charleston, SC
21 November 2010